I KNOW A LOT

FIRST CONCEPTS

Note:

To get the best learning out of this book, it is recommended that an adult join the fun and work with the child.

This edition published by Parragon Books Ltd in 2017 and distributed by

Parragon Inc.
440 Park Avenue South, 13th Floor
New York, NY 10016
www.parragon.com

Copyright © Parragon Books Ltd 2016-2017

Written by Susan Fairbrother and Andrea Turton
Illustrated by Emily Balsley, Abigail Burch, Beatrice Costamagna, Becky Down,
Abi Hall, Jannie Ho, Lauren Lowen, Emma Martinez, Hsinping Pan, Ana Seixas,
Hui Skipp, and Ruby Taylor
Cover illustrated by Olivier Latyk

ISBN 978-1-4748-9217-9

Printed in China

I
KNOW
A LOT

FIRST CONCEPTS

PaRragon

Bath • New York • Cologne • Melbourne • Delhi
Hong Kong • Shenzhen • Singapore

CONTENTS

1

2

NUMBERS

3

4

Lots of balloons!
Touch each balloon as you count them all.

1

2

3

4

5

1.

Just **1** of everything.

1 volcano ...

1 tree ...

1 big dino coming ... run, run, RUN!

8

1 sun ...

Draw **1** ladybug, **1** dragonfly, **1** bush, **1** rock, and **1** puddle!

Find **1** of each of these.

nest

flower

sun

volcano

cloud

Here is **1** smiling cat.

2:

Your turn ...

Now there are
2 smiling cats!

Whose boots?
Ready, draw!

2 boots make a pair ...
2 perfect pairs of boots!

Where's Barney? He's late!

How many bears are sitting on chairs?

123

3

Trace the lines.

Whee! It's number 3!

How many billy goats gruff found a safe way across the bridge? Count the clever goats.

ROAD CLOSED

How many passengers will the bus pick up altogether?

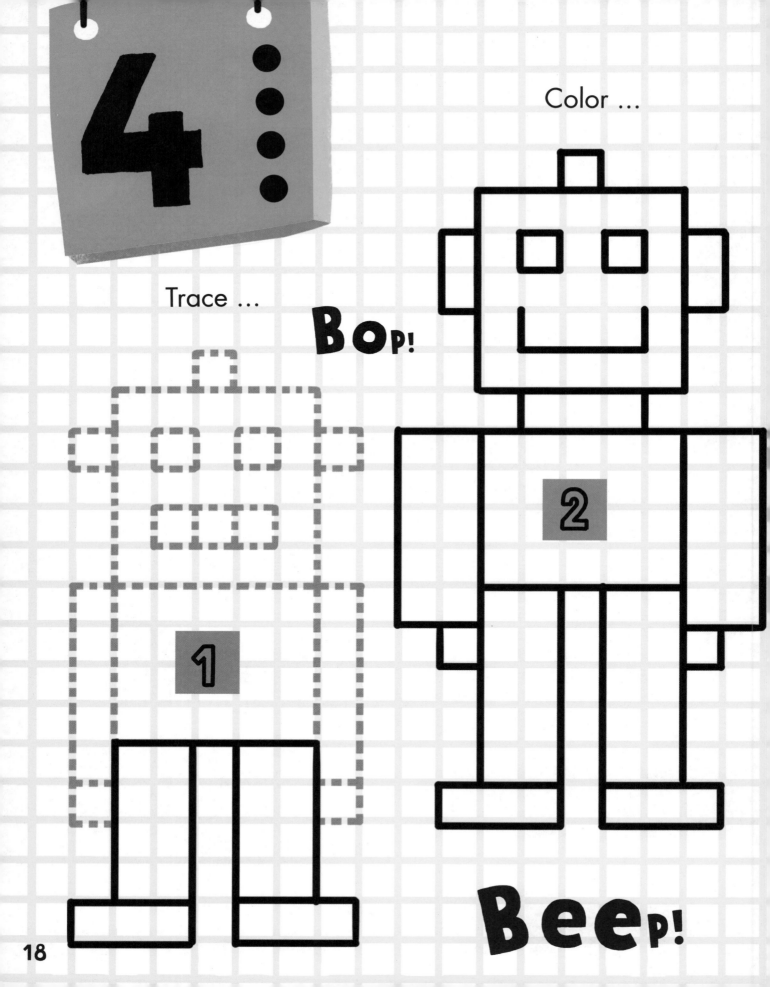

Color ...

4

Trace ...

BOP!

1

2

Beep!

18

Draw ...

Doodle!

BOOp!

4

3

BLip!

5 ⫶⫶

Magic beans for sale!
Price: **1** cow for **5** beans

Here's **1** cow.

Now draw Jack's **5** beans!

Draw **5** golden eggs in the nest.

Look at that beanstalk! Color it green.

Draw a magic bean at the bottom.

Color **5** red cars, **2** green cars, and **3** blue cars.

How many birds? Write the answers on the leaves.

1

6

Oink!

Roar!

The nose knows!
Whose noses are those?
Draw a face around each one.

Trumpet!

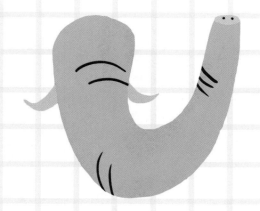

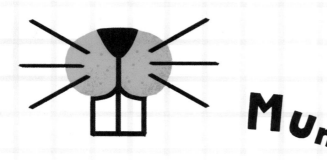

MUnch!

Ooh-ooh-aah-aah!

Squeak!

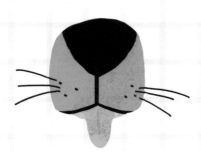

Woof!

27

Brrr!

28

Warm up chilly Octopus by drawing him **7** more cozy mittens.

8

That's better!

10

Draw and color the missing birds to make **5** groups of **10**!

That's really impressive!

Connect the dots to start the birthday party.

1
2
3
9
10
4
5
8
7
6

Wriggle the worm to the red apple.

1

3

2

4

8

5

7

6

9

10

Count the apples on the tree!

36

Follow the trail of this hungry snail.

How many of these can you count in the vegetable plot?

Connect the dots to
give each boat sails.

5 6

4

6 5 7

3

7 4 8

Ahoy, there!

8

2

3

9

1 10 9 2 1 10

Find **9** fish in
the sea.

How many birds
can you count?

1 2 3

10 hungry hamsters!

Draw **1** piece of food on each hamster's plate.

Star light, star bright!

How many yellow stars in the sky tonight?

42

This time, start at number 10 and join the dots backward!

Blast off!

Have you ever seen such a magnificent palace?

20 of everything, everywhere!

How many do you count?

Draw more to make **20** of each!

Connect the dots to make these racing cars **zoom!**

START

1
15
2
12
4
3
5
6
7
2
9
8
14
13
11
10

8
9
5
6
11
10
4
7
12
3
13
2
19
15
14
1
20
18
17
16

10 hens!

Count them and color the scenes.

1 hen here

1 hen in a car

3 hens on a bus

2 hens together

1 hen in bed

1 hen in a boat

1 hen in a den

10 hens in all!

COLORS

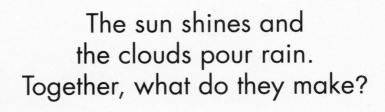

The sun shines and
the clouds pour rain.
Together, what do they make?

red

orange

yellow

green

blue

indigo

violet

A rainbow!

Color it in.

There are three main colors.
We call them **primary colors**.
Point to each color and say its name.

RED

YELLOW

BLUE

Doodle more things
for each color.

Red truck, **yellow** truck, **red** truck, **yellow** truck,

red truck,   **yellow** truck,   **red** truck,   **yellow** truck.

Circle the odd one out.
Finish the patterns in black below.

Answer:

White sheep ...

Change the white wool to black. Now they're all ...

... **black** sheep!

Baa, baa, baaaaa!

Arr!

Captain Yellowpeg loves anything **yellow**!
Circle 10 **yellow** things.

Here are Captain Redmane
and Captain Bluebeard, too!
Circle something **blue** and
something **red** for each of them.

These are **warm** colors.

What is your favorite warm color?
Draw something with that color here.

What is your favorite cool color?
Draw something with that color here.

Who's hiding where?
Write the number in the box.

Green frog
☐

Blue octopus
☐

Blue bird
☐

Orange cat
☐

1
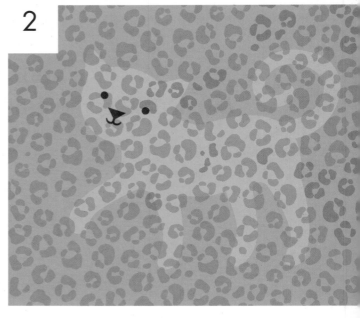

2
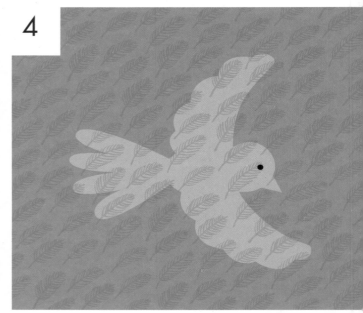

3

4

Zebra, Giraffe, Peacock, and Snake want to hide too!
Color each one to match the background.

Answer: Green frog – 3, Blue octopus – 1, Blue bird – 4, Orange cat – 2.

Color the clouds from light to dark ...

Light gray cloud.

Fluffy **white** cloud.

Little **black** clouds, ready to rain!

Big **dark gray** cloud.

Take cover!

What a lovely landscape!

Now go color crazy! Color the sky **purple** and the grass **pink**. Draw a **yellow** cloud, **blue** horses, and a **green** sun.

Sparkle and shine!

Jewel colors are deep, sparkling colors. They are named after precious stones.

ruby

emerald

sapphire

amber

amethyst

Draw lines to match each crown to its jewel name.

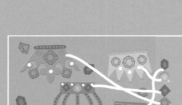

Which is your
favorite crown?

The aliens are ready to blast off!

Navy Blue

Sea Green

Chocolate Brown

Lemon Yellow

Coral Pink

Crimson

Trace the lines to take each rocket to its matching planet.

Warm Summer

Draw some warm summer things and cool winter things.

Cool Winter

All in **orange**!

pink and **purple**

Doodle in color to complete these patterns.

blue and **green**

shades of **blue**

red and **yellow**

Pick a color from the paintpots.
Doodle a picture using shades
of this color.

Now pick another color.
Doodle a picture using
shades of this color.

Color all the shadows **black**.

Color each cactus **green**.

It's sunset! Color the sky with warm **pinks** and **oranges.**

Now color the trees and animals in a dark color to stand out against the bright sunset.

78

black patches

red patches

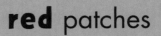

Draw matching colored patches on each cow.

light blue patches

dark blue patches

patches in **shades of blue**

light brown patches

What crazy colors!

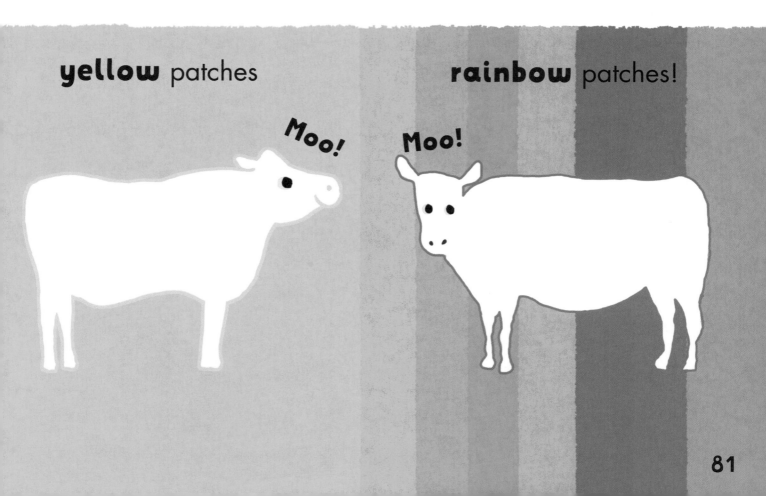

yellow patches

rainbow patches!

We're ready to land!
These runways are color coded.
Finish the words.

R__D

B__UE

__RANGE

P__RPLE

PI__K

YELLO___

GRE___N

WH___TE

B___ACK

GR___Y

Connect the dots to help the
flowers grow!

red

green

purple

84

85

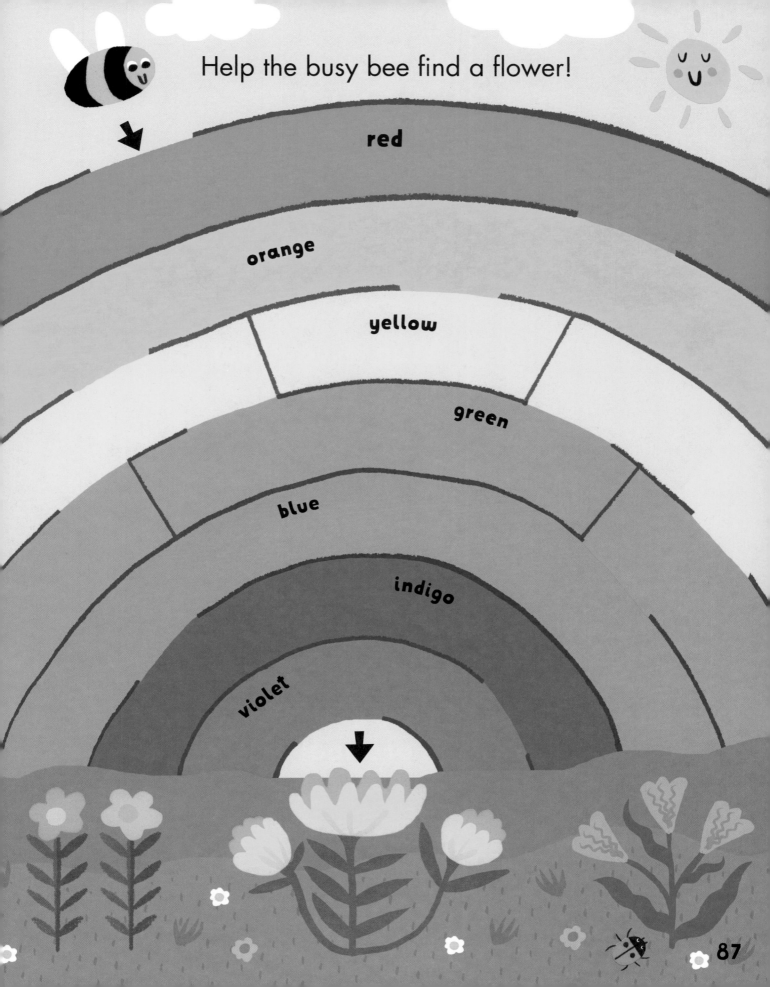

Help the busy bee find a flower!

red

orange

yellow

green

blue

indigo

violet

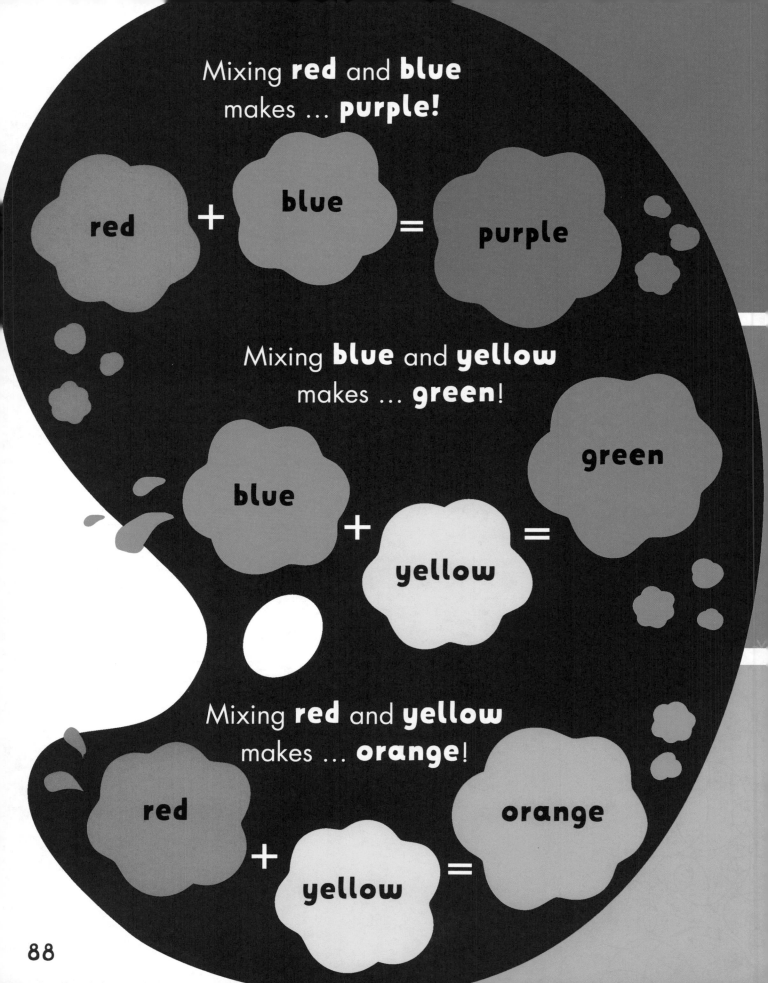

Mixing **red** and **blue**
makes ... **purple!**

red + blue = purple

Mixing **blue** and **yellow**
makes ... **green**!

blue + yellow = green

Mixing **red** and **yellow**
makes ... **orange**!

red + yellow = orange

Purple things! Finish the words.

 cr___wn

 g___apes

 flow___r

Green things! Finish the words.

 fr___g

 el___

 ___iwi

Orange things! Finish the words.

 c___t

 co___e

 ___ish

Color the flowers!

blue

orange

red

indigo

violet

yellow

green

90

tree

sun

car

WORDS

pencil

rabbit

butterfly

flower

frog

Look, a cloud that looks like a **cat**!
Doodle other objects you can see in the clouds.

cat

flower

umbrella

tree

hat

key

stop

What vehicles can you see? Doodle more cars.

car

tractor

bus

94

excavator

go

van

A sailor went to sea, sea, sea,
To see what she could see, see, see ...

bird

sail

boy

girl

map

fin

What can you see, see, see? Circle these objects in the picture, then check them here:

☐ **bell**

☐ **sun**

☐ **tree**

☐ **cat**

☐ **fish**

Hide-and-seek!

Find and trace the letters in the picture. Then write them here to complete these words.

_ **o g**

_ **a t**

_ **e n**

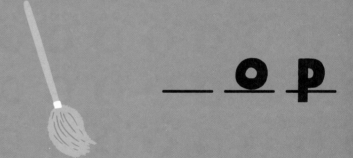
_ **o p**

Circle 7
red things.

boot

Fire Department

  fire truck

balloon

mug

hood

stop

hose

101

Finish the
animal words.

d___g on
a l___g

b___g on
a r___g

bir___ in
a n___st

___ox in
a b___x

f___og on
a l___g!

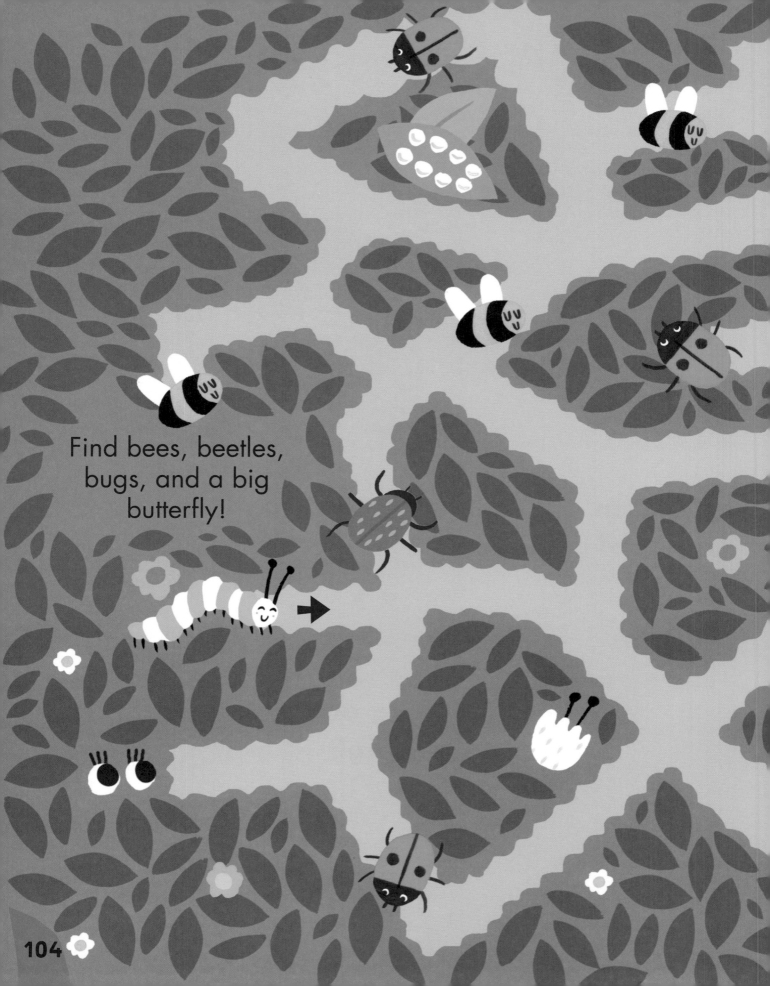

Find bees, beetles, bugs, and a big butterfly!

Doodle a cat on the **mat**.

cat

hat

Draw a pattern on the rat's **hat**.

rat

Doodle passengers on the **plane**.

cat • bat • mouse

Who's **snug** on the **rug**?

bug

107

These sharks love to make words!

big

fin

teeth

Find what we like to eat.

bone apple carrot

Welcome to the store of many things!

pots and pans

bags

mats

fans

Doodle more things in each room.

zippers

pets

wigs

mugs

113

Cute kittens!

They are ...

warm

~~slimy~~

cuddly

scaly

cold

soft

pink

116 Feed me!

Doodle things to feed the
monster and check as you go ...

smelly **cheese** and old **peas**

socks, **clocks**, and **rocks**

a **bat** and a **hat**

a **shell** and a **bell**

a **mug** and a **rug**!

Presents!

Draw a line between each bunny and her present.

Thank you for my **carrot**

Thank you for my **bun**

Thank you for
my **bear**

Thank you for
my **hat**

Thank you for
my **bell**

Connect the dots with the bears on the beach.

121

Does the cat look ...

happy

or

sad?

Circle the right word.

He's sad!
He wants a
makeover.

How about
a **hat**?

A **cap**? A **crown**?

No? How about a big **grin**!

Draw it on.
That's better!

king

Who is wearing
these crowns?

queen

Match the pictures to the words!

dog

tree

frog

hat

cat

car

hen

moon

sock

shell

bell

a b c d e f g h i j k l m

Start with the letter **a** to connect these dots.

126

Get the frog to his log.

Ribbit!

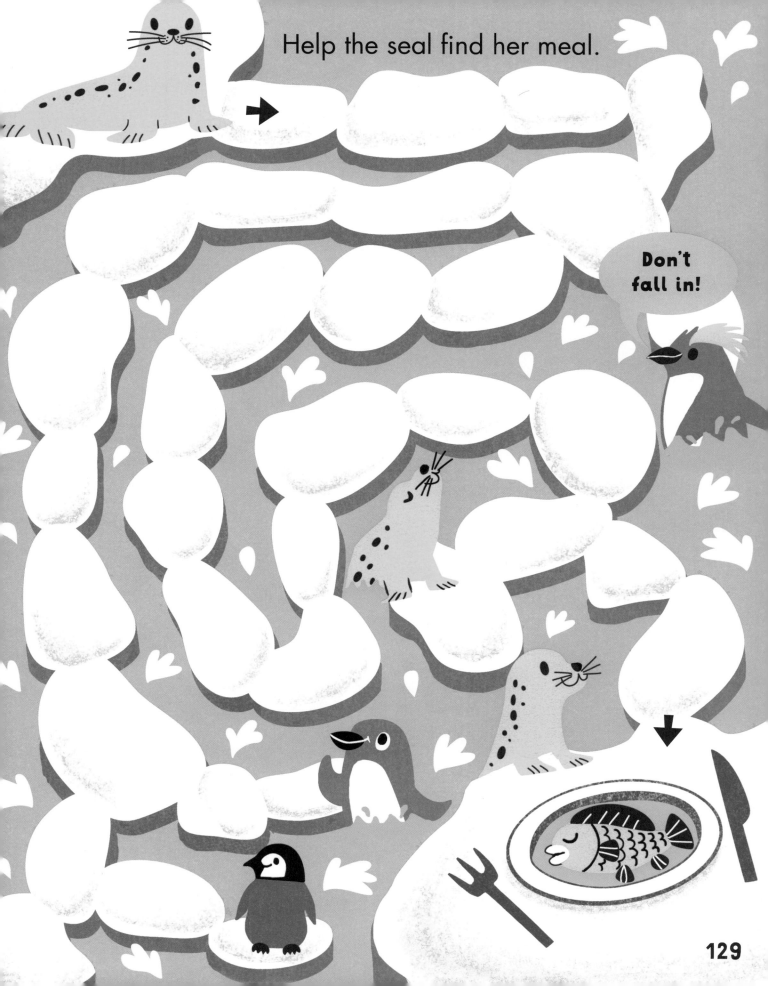

Help the seal find her meal.

Don't fall in!

129

What's the weather today?
Draw.

rain
Make it wet.

Doodle.

wind
Make it blow.

Color.

sun
Make it hot.

Trace.

snow
Make it cold.

Pigs **LOVE** mud.
Draw some splats.

pig

mud

Now doodle some bubbles to clean them up in the **tub**!

SHAPES

Let's dance!
Trace and try these moves.

Try little steps
in a **circle**.

Yee haw! Make
a **square**!

Color the white
shapes on the
dancers.

Try a
triangle!

Tippity tap a **star** shape!

Dance in a dazzling **diamond**!

Bravo!

Glide across the floor in a **rectangle**.

135

Snail only eats round lettuce!
Connect the **circles** to help her
munch her way across the garden.

Start

Munch! Crunch!

Finish

Point to a **huge** rabbit! Find
3 **teeny-tiny** bunnies, too.

Lots of shapes can make pretty patterns. Finish these!

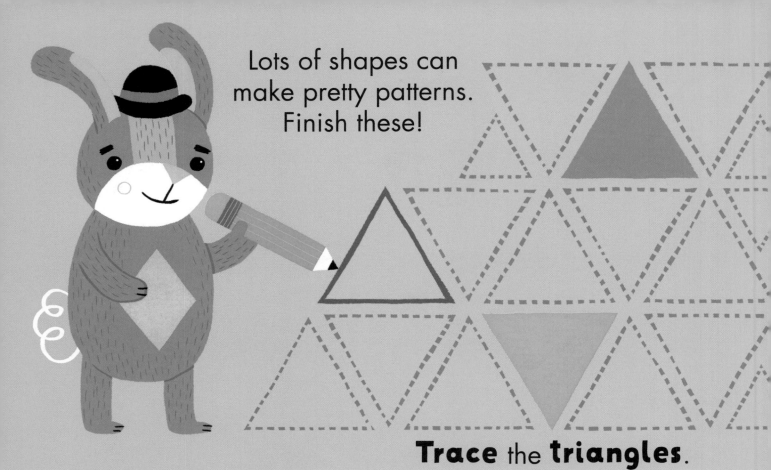

Trace the **triangles**.

Color the **diamonds**.

Draw more **circles**.

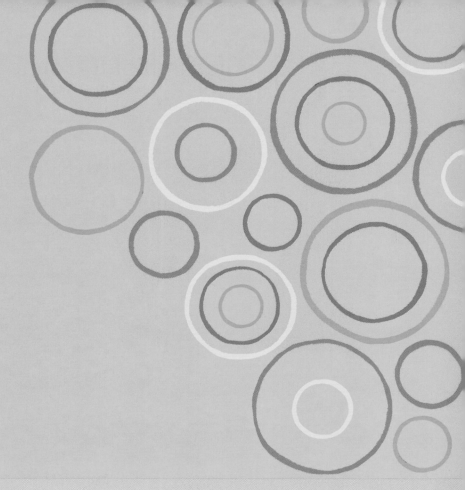

Doodle some **squares**!

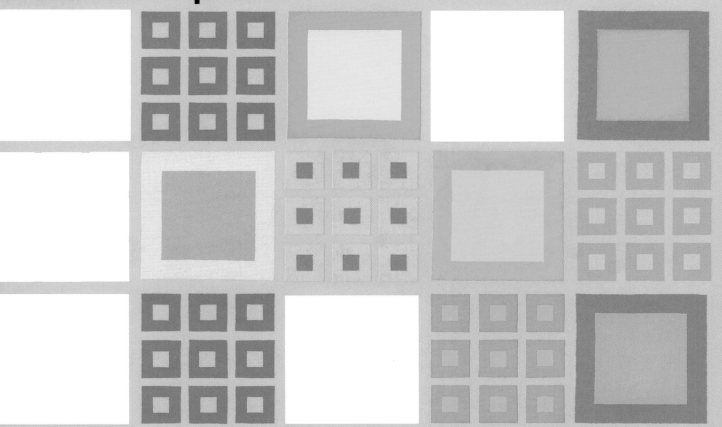

Kites in flight! Connect the dots.

Tick, tock!
Finish the clock.

How many?

rectangle

square

triangle

circle

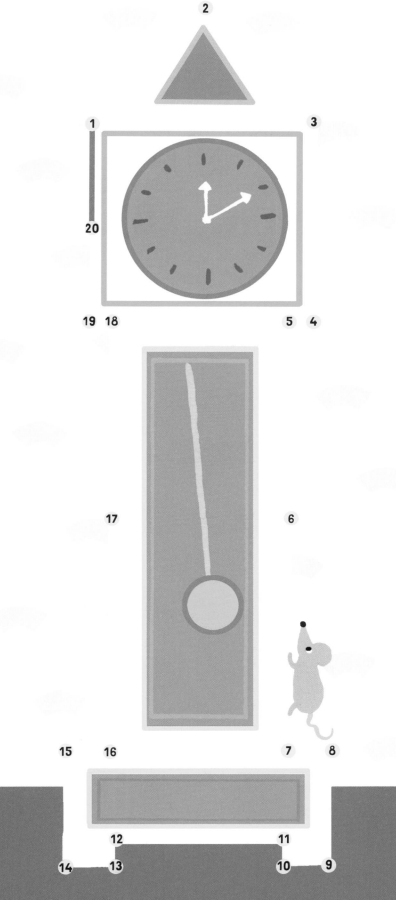

The **Circle** Restaurant!
Draw circle-shaped food
on the round plates.

What doesn't belong here?
Find three foods that aren't
circle-shaped.

Look at the **stars** in the sky.
Color lots more!

Trace the dotted lines to fill the sky with shooting stars!

145

Welcome to the shape store.
How can we help you today?

Rectangles

St__rs

S__uares

How many shapes can you name?
Finish the words.

Ci__cles

Trian__les

Find one of each of these items in the store, then check them off your list!
A shape with ...

3 sides and **3 corners**

1 curved side

4 sides all the **same length**

4 sides: **2 longer** ones and **2 shorter** ones

Shiver me timbers, it's Captain Squarebeard! Can you spot the shapes he's buried on the island?

148

Draw lines to match
these whole shapes
to the buried ones.

square

circle

triangle

rectangle

star

149

lots of
circles

just one
circle

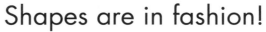
Shapes are in fashion!

narrow
triangles

wide
triangles

stars on top

stars on the bottom

Color all the shapes.

lots of **squares**!

T. rex has eaten parts
of these shapes!
Color in the missing pieces.

152

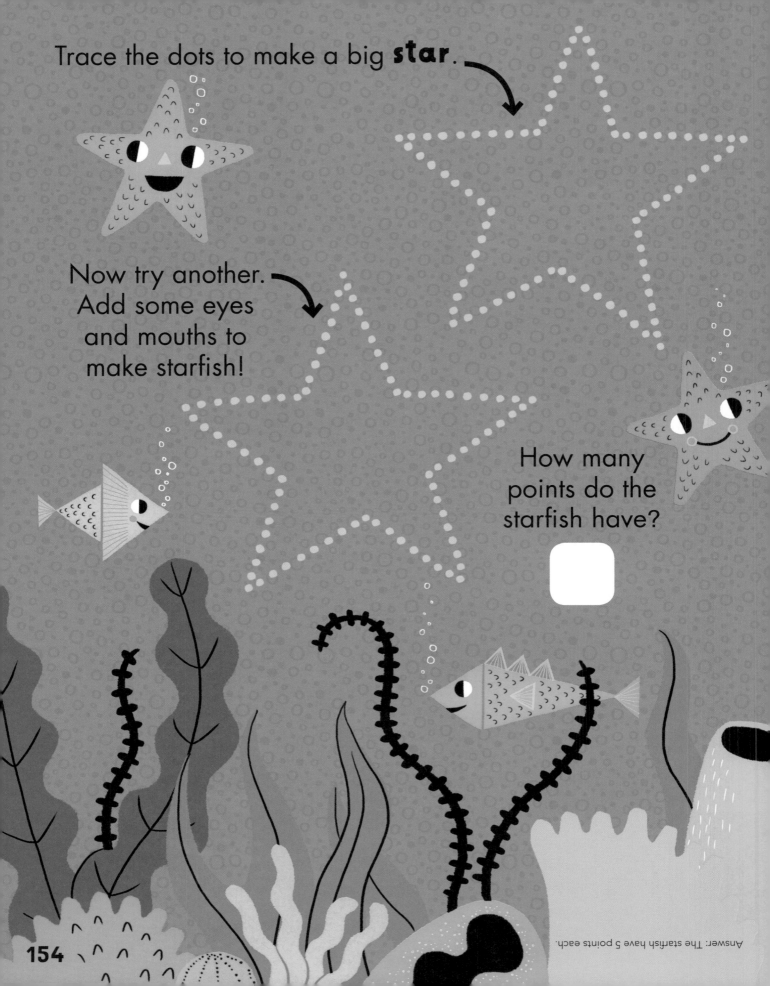

Trace the dots to make a big **star**.

Now try another. Add some eyes and mouths to make starfish!

How many points do the starfish have?

Starfish love silly star glasses!

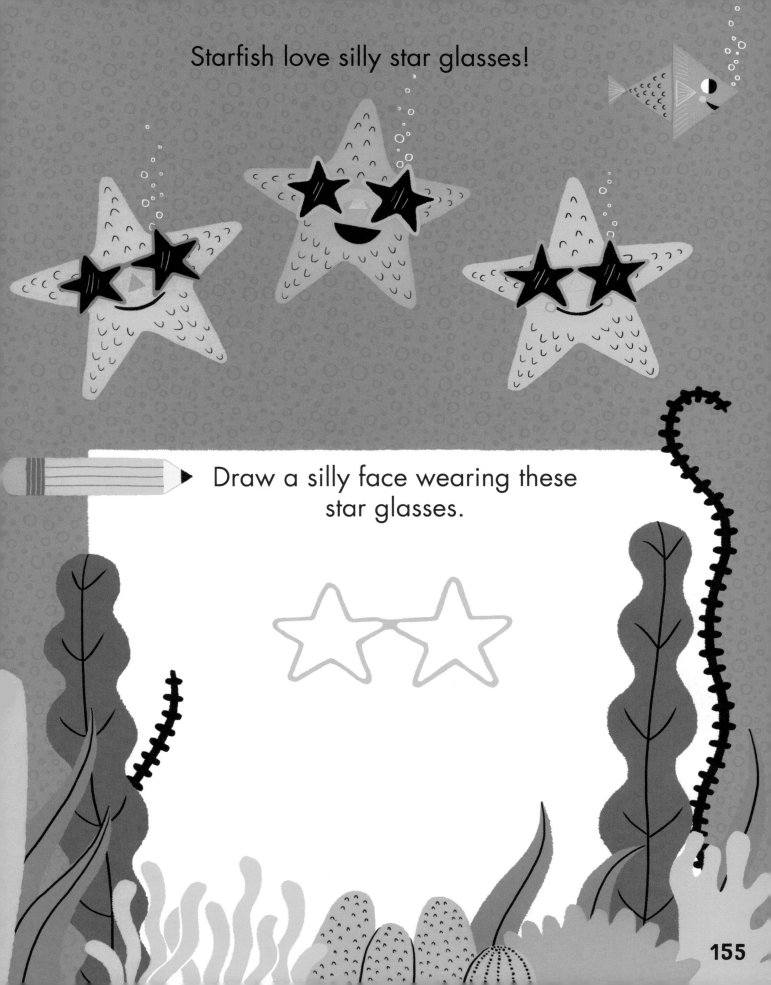

Draw a silly face wearing these star glasses.

Speedy spiders spinning webs.

Around and around I go!

156

How many?

hexagon   square   triangle **157**

It's a big parking lot!

Shape City!

Doodle more cars in the **rectangle** spaces.

GO

How many other shapes can you see?

○ **circles**

_____

△ **triangles**

_____

☆ **stars**

_____

Some shapes aren't flat.
We call them **3D** shapes!

Each kite has a
different 3D shape.
Whose is whose and
which is which? Trace
the strings to find out.

160

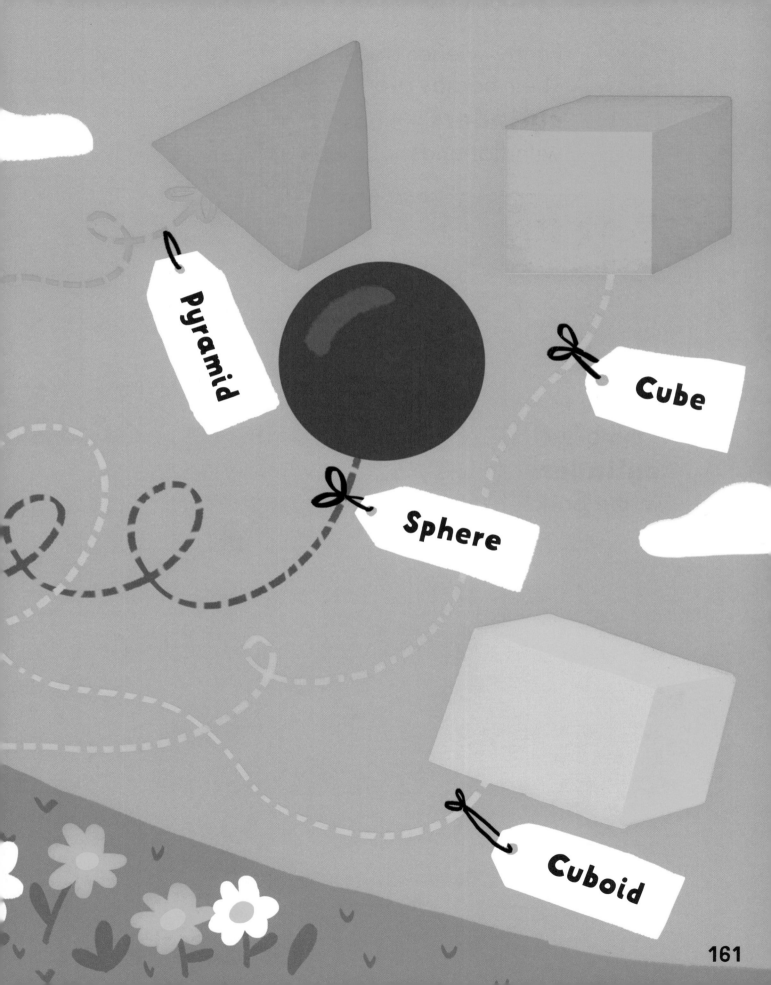

Pyramid

Cube

Sphere

Cuboid

Funny wiener dogs! Their bodies are **cylinders**—tubes with flat ends.

Point to the other **cylinders** in the park.

Have no fear, Super **Sphere** is here! A **sphere** has no corners.

Draw some more **spheres** here.

A ball is a **sphere**.

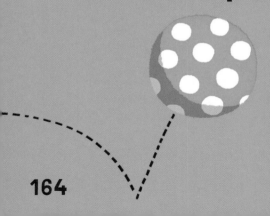

So is the moon!

 Welcome to the **cone** zone! Cones come to a point.

Make sure everyone has a party-hat **cone** and an ice-cream **cone**! Draw them on.

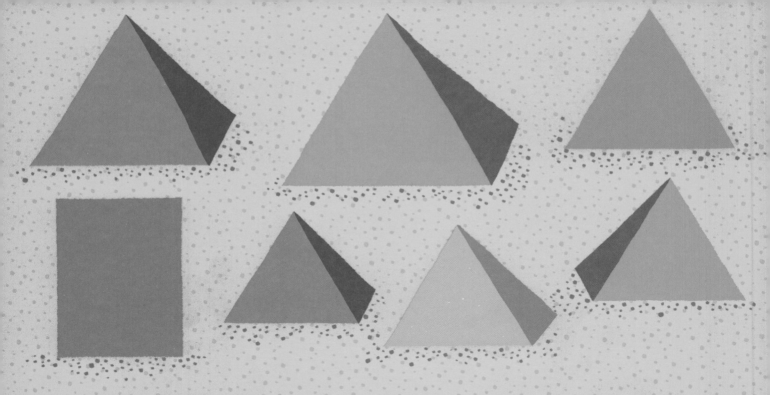

Pyramids have sloping sides and come to a point.
Which shapes here are not **pyramids** at all? Circle them.

166

Shape safari!
Keep your
eyes peeled.

168

What can you spot?

☐ cubes

☐ rectangles

☐ cylinders

☐ diamonds

☐ triangles

☐ circles

Let's make some shape people!
Give them smiley faces.

Draw on some arms and legs!

Look at the patterns to help each baby dino find its daddy.

Draw the shapes in their frames.

square

circle

triangle

star

rectangle

diamond

sphere

pyramid

cube

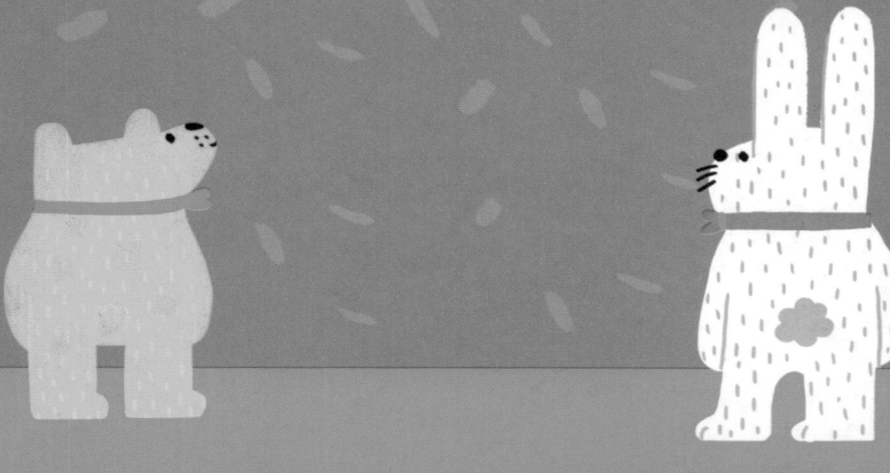

happy

sad

hot

cold

OPPOSITES

little

big

tall

short

How do you feel today?
Draw your **happy** face.

What makes you **happy**?

Check if the
faces are
happy and
cross if they
are sad.

176

Draw your **sad** face.

What makes you **sad**?

Trace to make these **short** things **long**.

True or False?
Check to show which are **true**.
Cross to show which are **false**.

 Dogs go **MOO!**

 Cows go **MOO!**

 Tomatoes are **BLUE**.

 Tomatoes are **RED**.

Answer: False, True, False, True.

Watch out, it's very wobbly at the **top**!

Draw some eye-catching outfits on the acrobats—use spots and stripes!

It's safer at the **bottom!**

Find these things, then check them here!

A pig in a wig ⚪

A rat with a hat ⚪

A cat with a bat ⚪

A fox in a box ⚪

Who lives where? Trace and color the bird **high** up in the sky and the fish down **low** in the sea.

below

above

Doodle some friends for them **above** and **below** the waves.

It's the **lost** and **found** office. Follow the lines to match the lost things to their owners.

LOST AND FOUND

The queen has **lost** her crown jewels!
Doodle them for her—you **found** them!

Uh-oh! Construction EVERYWHERE!
Can you help Mr. Bear find his way home?

How many green **GO** signs can you see? ☐

How many red **STOP** signs are there? ☐

Welcome to the **Opposites** Store!
How can we help you today?

Find these opposites in the store, then check them off your list.

big and **small**

open and **closed**

happy and **sad**

empty and **full**

189

This little mouse loves to explore.
Find her in the **loud** city and the **quiet** countryside.

It's **loud** in the city!

Color all the noisy cars.

beep beep

Find two more **loud** things in the sky.

It's **quiet** in the countryside!

Finish coloring the scene ... **shh**!

tweet tweet

Find two **quiet** butterflies.

191

This is the house of a
very forgetful mouse.

upstairs

Help the mouse find these objects in the house. Draw an **up** or a **down** arrow to show her whether they are **upstairs** or **downstairs**.

downstairs

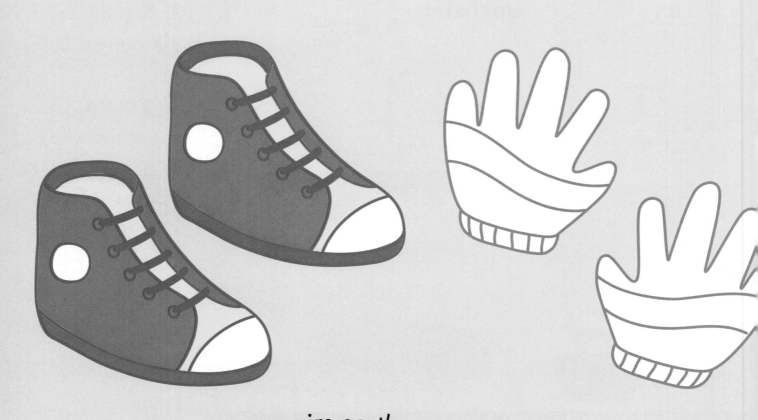

Color these pairs so they all look the **same**.

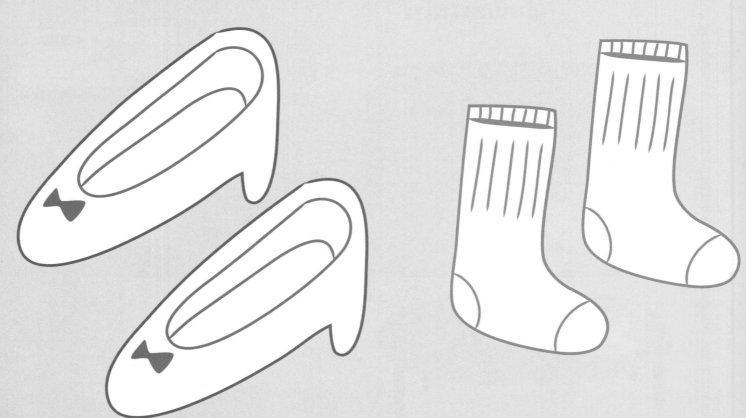

194

Color these pairs so they all look **different**.

The alien spaceships need to get home to their planet.

Follow the trails with your finger—which is **straight** and which is **bendy**?

196

3 spaceships fly **straight** to Earth.
2 spaceships take a **bendy** route.
Draw the trails.

Red Riding Hood is **inside** the house.

Who's **outside** the house?

outside

inside

Rapunzel is **inside** the castle.

Who's **outside** the castle?

inside

outside

over

under

The prince is **over** the sea.

Who's **under** the sea?

The billy goat is **over** the bridge.

Who's **under** the bridge?

over

under

These **small** animals are lost.
Can you find a matching **big** animal for each one?

Draw
lines to
match the
pairs.

Find and tick these **big** and **small** things.

201

Phew—riding up the hill is **slow**!

Whee—rolling down the hill is **fast!**

Doodle more people going **up** and **down** the steep hill.

High in the trees!

Squawk!

204

Connect the dots!

Low on the ground!

Who is **heavy** and who is **light**?

Circle all the **light** things.
Now circle the **heavy** things
in a different color.

Draw something **heavy** here to try to balance the seesaw.

Can you match all these opposites?

clean

closed

full

dirty

open

smooth

rough

front

back

empty

Answer: clean and dirty, full and empty, open and closed, rough and smooth, back and front.

stop

sad

new

small

big

cold

happy

go

hot

old

Connect the dots to see who's making a new friend!

You're very **small.**

And you're very **tall!**

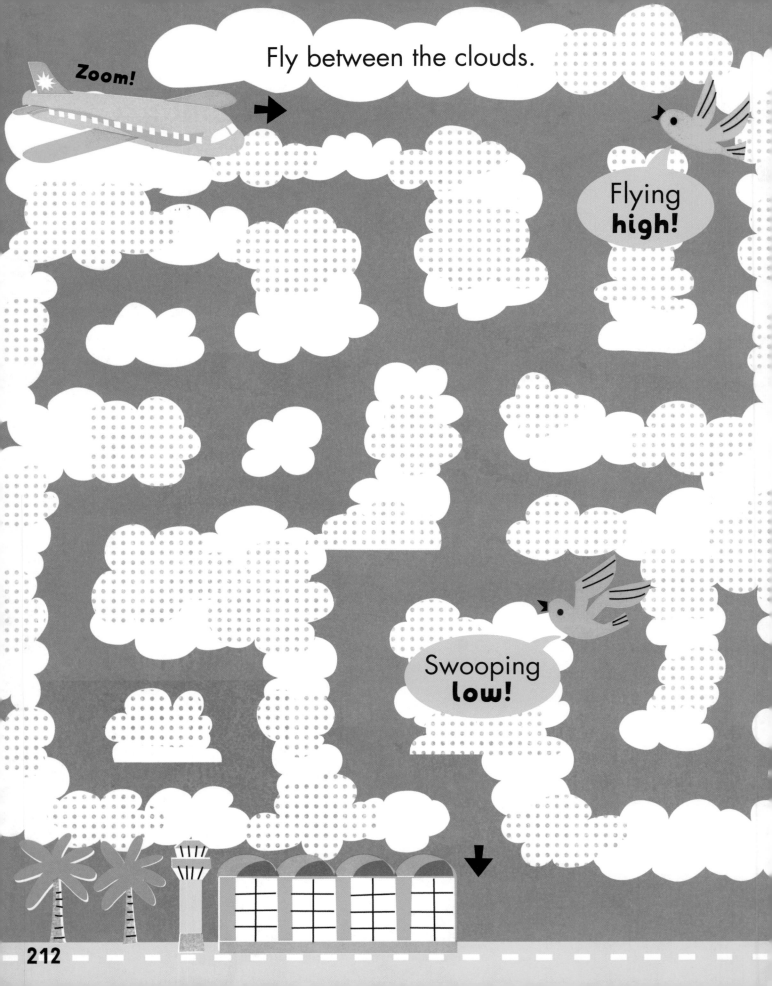

We're at the **top** ...
ready to splash at
the **bottom**!

213

Opposites Camp!
Big and little

big

little

Find and check the opposites!

big car ☐

little car ☐

big tent ☐

little tent ☐

big fire ☐

little fire ☐

big pan ☐

little pan ☐

big kettle ☐

little kettle ☐

big flower ☐

little flower ☐

big butterfly ☐

little butterfly ☐

215

STORIES

Once upon a time ...

Three bears and three chairs ...
Circle all the other groups of three.

Can you find Goldilocks in the picture? Circle her.

Cinderella is dreaming of going to the ball.

Doodle to make her dream come true.

Here's Prince Charming!

Trace the dots to see Cinderella's glass slipper.

What's the story?

Number the circles to put the frames in the correct order.

Follow the path that leads the three little pigs to their safe brick house.

A B C

log

tree

Rapunzel, Rapunzel! Let down your hair!
Which braid leads to the fairytale prince?

A

B

C

224

Rapunzel's hair is ...

Circle the four words that
describe Rapunzel's hair.

blonde

long

purple

curly

short

spiky

green

straight   shiny

dull

What can you spot?

Find the **bold** words in the picture.

One day, far out in the ocean, a band of pirates was sailing the seas searching for **treasure.** Suddenly, the captain held up his **map** and pointed ... "There it is! X marks the spot!" The **pirate ship** sailed full speed ahead toward the island. But the treasure was guarded by a fierce **crocodile**!

Draw below what you think happens next.

What a treat! A house made of candy.
Doodle more sugary treats.

Count and write how many candies each child eats!

Hansel is really hungry and he eats all these candies.

Gretel has a sweet tooth and she eats all these candies.

Fee Fi Fo Fum ...
Here comes a giant—run, Jack, run!

"Hurry, Jack!"

Find a way down through the beanstalk maze so Jack can escape from the giant ... quickly!

"My, what big feet you have, Granny!"

Little Red Riding Hood loves the color ... red!
Circle 10 red things in the picture.

Eek! That's not Granny—it's the wolf!
Can you find the real Granny? Circle her.

Oh no! It's the big bad wolf!

Quick—build the three little pigs a
safe house by doodling more bricks.

"Eeek!"

What is the wolf saying? Fill in the missing words.

I'll _____ and
I'll _____ and I'll _____
your _____ down!

blow

huff

puff

house

Fairytale Forest

Help the princess find her way to her castle. What does she see along the way?

princess

wizard

cave

wolf

giant

troll

witch

fairy

castle

Run, run as fast as you can!
Decorate the gingerbread man to bring him to life.

Fill in the missing letters.
Cross off each letter you use.

R__n, run as fast as you can.

Y__u can't catch m__ ,

I'm the g__ngerbread m__n!

a

e

i

o

u

Look closely!
Can you spot 10 differences between these pictures?

Trace a number each time you find a difference.

1 2 3 4 5 6

"Don't boast about your lightning pace,
for slow and steady won the race!"

7 8 9 10

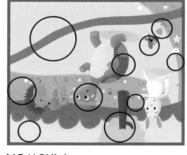

What a pair!

These two kind elves are helping the poor shoemakers.

Doodle to finish the patterns on the shoes below.

Draw lines to match the pairs.

It's Snow White's dwarfs!
Circle the correct word
to describe these dwarfs.

asleep   awake

happy   sad

grumpy   cheerful

big   small

Count and color 7 dwarfs.

1 one

2 two

3 three

4 four

5 five

6 six

7 seven

What comes next?

Doodle to finish the sequence on each mattress.

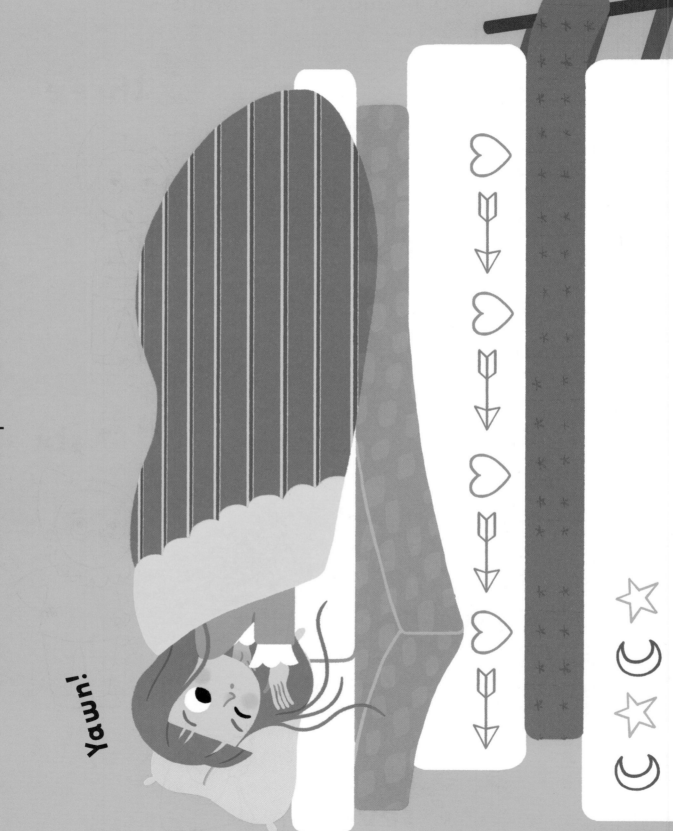

Yawn!

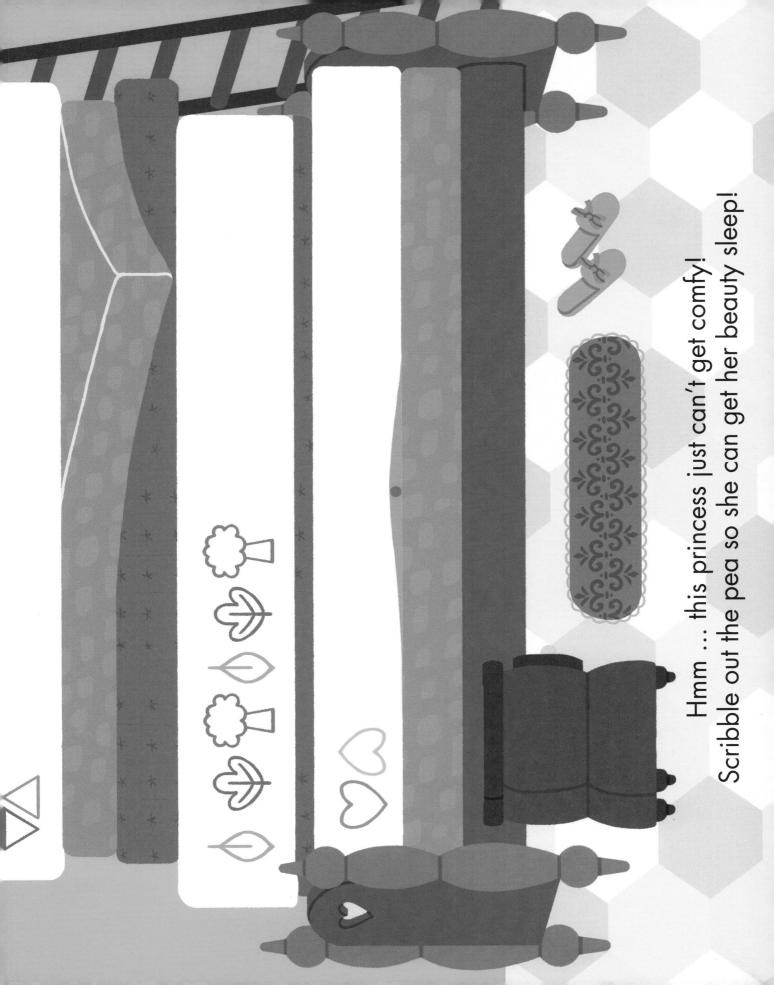

Hmm ... this princess just can't get comfy!
Scribble out the pea so she can get her beauty sleep!

Once upon a time ...

Pick your favorite fairytale characters and create a story.
Draw what happens in the boxes below.

Write the title here:

....

Remember to give it a beginning, a middle, and a happy ending!

The Little Mermaid is looking out to sea.
What can she see?

Find all of these sea creatures in the picture.

8 sea horses

10 fish

6 crabs

1 dolphin

Check the boxes as you go!

Whoosh!

Zoom! Zoom!
Which way to
the moon?

Blast through the galaxy to planet Earth.

Connect the dots to finish
building the castle.